Pass the Pepper Please!

Healthy Meal Planning for People on Sodium Restricted Diets

DIANE READER, R.D.
MARION FRANZ, M.S., R.D.

Introduction by Richard Bergenstal, M.D.

Table of Contents

Cover & text design: Terry Dugan Design
Cover & test illustrations: Terry Dugan
Typesetting: Dahl & Curry
Printing: Monotrade Companies

International Diabetes Center
©1988

Library of Congress Cataloging-in-Publication Data

Reader, Diane.
   Pass the pepper please!
   (The Wellness & Nutrition Library)
   Includes bibliographies and index.
   1. Salt-free diet—Recipes. I. Franz, Marion J.
II. Title. III. Title: Healthy meal planning for people on sodium
restricted diets. IV. Series. [DNLM: 1. Cookery. 2. Diet, Sodium-
Restricted—popular works. 3. Hypertension—prevention &
control—popular works.
WB 424 R286p]
RM237.8.43 1987 641.5'632 87-20209
ISBN 0-937721-17-4

Published by Diabetes Center, Inc.
P.O. Box 739
Wayzata, Minnesota 55391

Printed in the United States of America.

Acknowledgements

The authors wish to thank the dietitians of the International Diabetes Center — Gay Castle, Nancy Cooper, Broatch Haig, Arlene Monk, and Gretchen Morin — for their assistance in putting this book together. Thanks also to Tom Slack, M.D.; Barb Hamilton, R.N.; and Liz Applegate, Ph.D. for reviewing the manuscript and making important suggestions. We would also like to thank Neysa C.M. Jensen and Donna R. Hoel for their help in editing the book and Terry Dugan for illustrations and design. Finally, thank you to the entire staff of the IDC for their support and encouragement.

If you find this book helpful and would like more information on this and other related subjects you may be interested in one or more of the following titles from our *Wellness and Nutrition Library.*

BOOKS

The Joy of Snacks — Good Nutrition for People Who Like to Snack
                        (270 pages)
The Physician Within (176 pages)
Pass The Pepper Please (90 pages)
Fast Food Facts (56 pages)
Convenience Food Facts (210 pages)
Opening The Door To Good Nutrition (186 pages)
Learning to Live Well With Diabetes (392 pages)
Exchanges For All Occasions (210 pages)
A Guide To Healthy Eating (60 pages)

BOOKLETS & PAMPHLETS

Diabetes & Alcohol (4 Pages)
Diabetes & Excercise (20 pages)
Emotional Adjustment To Diabetes (16 pages)
Healthy Footsteps For People With Diabetes (13 pages)
Diabetes Record Book (68 pages)
Diabetes & Brief Illness (8 pages)
Diabetes & Impotence: A Concern for Couples (6 pages)
Adding Fiber To Your Diet (10 pages)
Gestational Diabetes: Guidelines for A Safe Pregnancy and Healthy Baby
                        (24 pages)
Recognizing and Treating Insulin Reactions (4 pages)
Hypoglycemia (functional) (4 pages)

The *Wellness and Nutrition Library* is published by Diabetes Center, Inc. in Minneapolis, Minnesota, publishers of quality educational materials dealing with health, wellness, nutrition, diabetes and other chronic illnesses. All our books and materials are available nationwide and in Canada through leading bookstores. If you are unable to find our books at your favorite bookstore contact us directly for a free catalog.

Diabetes Center, Inc.
P.O. Box 739
Wayzata, MN 55391

Introduction

Americans are becoming more health conscious all the time. We hear we should lose weight; eat less fat, salt, and sugar; eat more carbohydrates and fiber; take this or that vitamin; exercise more. How can we possibly make all of these changes? Our lifestyles are busy; our time is in demand. It's easy to know what is good for us, but it's hard to put that knowledge into practice.

That's why *Pass the Pepper Please!* was written. It provides some practical, easy-to-follow guidelines for reducing the salt (more specifically, sodium) in your diet.

Why is sodium "bad" for you? It is one of the risk factors associated with high blood pressure (hypertension), a disease that affects 60 million Americans and is the third leading cause of death in this country.

We at the International Diabetes Center are particularly concerned about hypertension. As you will read later in this book, hypertension is two to three times more common in adults with diabetes than in the general population. Hypertension can aggravate the very health conditions people with diabetes are at risk of developing—heart attacks, strokes, circulatory problems, and kidney and eye disease. That's why we tend to monitor and treat any elevation in blood pressure in these people very aggressively.

Fortunately, Americans seem to be becoming more aware of the serious consequences of uncontrolled hypertension. In a 1973 survey, 29 percent of those polled stated that high blood pressure causes stroke, and 24 percent believed high blood pressure was a factor in heart disease. A similar health survey in 1985 showed that 77 percent of the public knew high blood pressure was a factor in stroke, and 91 percent correctly stated that hypertension increases the chance of heart disease.

In addition, surveys have shown that more and more individuals are aware they have high blood pressure and have begun a treatment plan. Once you begin treatment, it's easy to assume that it must be working. Sometimes this is a mistaken assumption. As a matter of fact, one study found that 92 percent of individuals being treated for hypertension believed their blood pressure was controlled, but when blood pressure was actually measured, only about 24 percent of people being treated had achieved control.

The first part of this book will help you better understand what causes high blood pressure, how blood pressure is measured, and what is considered normal blood pressure. The consequences of not achieving your target blood pressure are also discussed.

All too often, a doctor's office visit, a community health screening program, or other health education books will leave you stuck in this first stage: you are aware you have high blood pressure and you need to be treating it effectively. *Pass the Pepper Please!* takes you beyond that phase by providing useful information to help you adopt health practices (particularly reducing sodium intake) that will help you actually achieve your goal of blood pressure control.

There are many things you can do to help control your blood pressure besides taking medications. Lifestyle changes to lower blood pressure include weight reduction, moderation in alcohol consumption, modifying dietary fat intake, avoiding tobacco, increasing exercise, and modifying behavior, perhaps through biofeedback or relaxation therapy. And, as you may know, a moderate salt restriction may significantly reduce high blood pressure.

What you may not know, and what is so clearly covered step-by-step in *Pass the Pepper Please!*, is exactly HOW to limit your sodium intake. You will learn how much sodium you currently consume compared with what you actually need. You will also see how much sodium is in various foods — a shocking revelation! Equally important are tips on how to choose lower sodium foods that fit into a healthy and enjoyable diet.

Lifestyle changes alone may not be enough to lower blood pressure, and you may have to take medication. There are many blood pressure-lowering pills available today. Your doctor must take into account your individual needs. If you are elderly, have diabetes or asthma, have elevated blood fats (cholesterol), or have heart pain (angina), your doctor will want to tailor the medication to your specific needs.

If you need to make changes in your life to improve your health, you are not alone. It's encouraging to know that the diet we recommend for people with hypertension or other health problems such as diabetes is the same one we recommend for all Americans. We can all benefit from eating less salt, exercising more, and taking care of our bodies.

We hope this book will help you in a practical way to reduce the amount of sodium you eat. You will feel better, and you will enjoy the real taste of your food more than ever. Here's to a life filled with new and exciting tastes!

Richard M. Bergenstal, M.D.
Associate Director of the International Diabetes Center

Pass the Pepper Please!

Have you been told you have high blood pressure?

Do you wonder what that means?

Do you wonder what caused it?

Do you wonder why you should be concerned about it?

Has your doctor told you to stop using salt?

If you answered yes to any of these questions, this book is for you. It will explain what high blood pressure is — or hypertension as your doctor calls it — why it's dangerous, and most important, what you can do about it. It will also explain why your doctor told you to stop using salt, which foods you can eat, and which foods to avoid.

Lest we confuse you right off the bat, we'll tell you a bit about the difference between salt and sodium.

Regular table salt is made up of sodium and chloride. (Maybe you remember the symbol NaCl from high school chemistry.) It's the sodium in salt that seems to cause problems for many of us. New studies show that the sodium and chloride combination also may be important in hypertension. No doubt we'll be hearing more about this.

If you look at a teaspoon of salt, you can figure about half of it is sodium and the rest is chloride. The average American eats 2 to 3 teaspoons of salt a day. That's roughly 8,000 milligrams of sodium. We'd all be far better off cutting back to about 3,000 milligrams of sodium — or approximately 1 teaspoon of salt. That may still seem like a lot, but as you will soon discover, or may have already discovered, it's difficult to restrict your sodium intake much more than that. Most of the salt we eat is well disguised in food and drink.

On the other hand, cutting down on salt doesn't mean you have to eat bland food. Nor does limiting salt or sodium intake necessarily mean limiting your food choices. This book will show you a wide variety of foods you can eat, plus spices you can use to add flavor to your food without adding salt or sodium. We hope you'll find this an exciting challenge—a chance to explore the use of a variety of new spices and tastes.

It's encouraging to know our taste for salty foods is not something we come by naturally, as is our taste for sweetness. While we are born with the ability to taste salt, the preference for salt develops only after we have been exposed to salty foods.

Back in 1916, the Diamond Crystal Salt Company published a booklet titled *One Hundred and One Uses for Salt*. It described how to use salt to poach eggs, keep vegetables green, make gravy, judge whether a mushroom is poisonous, and remove scales from fish. The company was educating and conditioning people to use salt.

See Use No. 58, Page II.

The booklet also describes uses for salt outside the kitchen. Some of them are quite humorous:

> *"60. To Kill Weeds: Obnoxious weeds may be killed by covering the stalks with salt. Salt may be used to keep down weeds by sprinkling it over the ground."*

> *"42. To Clean Brass and Copper: For cleaning brass and copper, there is nothing better than salt mixed with an equal amount of flour, and vinegar enough to make a paste. Let this remain on for an hour or so, then rub off with a soft cloth, afterwards washing and using a soft brush for places that cannot be reached with a cloth. Polish with a soft, dry, clean cloth."*

The introduction to this little book tells the housewife of 1916 that all good cooks use salt: "My old Aunt Samanthy used to say—and my, what a cook she was!—she used to say that getting married without love was like trying to cook without salt.

'If you forgits that little pinch of salt afore you boils your 'tatters,' she'd say, 'they never do taste right—no matter how much you salts 'em arterwards.'"

Fortunately, our preference for salt can be unlearned, just as it was learned. As you use less salt, you'll probably find foods you once liked will taste too salty. Perhaps you've discovered that already.

Hypertension

Part I

What is hypertension?

Hypertension is a serious health problem affecting about 60 million Americans—or about one of every four people. If you're one of those 60 million, you undoubtedly have had a lot of questions about hypertension and why you should be concerned about it.

Blood pressure is the force pushing blood through the body's circulatory system. High blood pressure, or hypertension, occurs when blood pushes against the walls of the arteries with extreme force.

Hypertension does not mean you are nervous or tense. Calm and relaxed people can have high blood pressure.

Why should you be concerned about hypertension?

Because hypertension puts extra strain on the heart, it's an important risk factor in coronary heart and blood vessel disease. Two other important risk factors are high blood cholesterol levels and smoking.

Untreated or uncontrolled high blood pressure contributes, over time, to:

- coronary artery disease (chest pains—angina or heart attack)
- congestive heart failure (a condition in which the heart fails to pump properly, causing a backlog of blood that can congest the lungs and cause shortness of breath)
- cerebrovascular accidents (a stroke due to a decrease in the blood supply to the brain)
- kidney disease (the kidneys cannot properly filter wastes from the body).

Hypertension is called "the silent killer." It rarely produces warning signals, yet it can lead to serious problems.

If you have diabetes, you need to be particularly careful about hypertension, since it's two to three times more common in people with diabetes than in the general population. Because of your diabetes, you're already at a greater risk than the general population for heart disease, stroke, and small blood vessel diseases that can damage the kidneys and the eyes. Because all of these problems are affected by hypertension, you need to do everything you can to prevent high blood pressure. If it does develop, it must be treated early and aggressively.

How do you know you have high blood pressure?

Blood pressure is measured using a device called a sphygmomanometer. That's the technical name for the inflatable cuff, bulb, and dial or column of mercury so familiar to many of us. The person taking your blood pressure places the cuff on your arm, inflates it, and then lets air out of the cuff while listening through a stethoscope to the sound of the blood passing through the artery.

Blood pressure is always recorded as two measurements. The first is the systolic pressure, which is the pressure against the blood vessel wall while the heart is contracting. The second is the diastolic pressure, which is the pressure as the heart is relaxing and filling with blood before it contracts again.

The goal for healthy adults is approximately 120 mm Hg (millimeters of mercury) systolic and 80 mm Hg diastolic. You will see the blood pressure written as systolic over diastolic, for example — 120/80. If you forget which is which, remember: <u>d</u>iastolic is <u>d</u>own.

There's no absolute point that clearly separates normal pressure from abnormal. However, blood pressure levels above 140 mm Hg systolic and/or 90 mm Hg diastolic are considered high and require medical attention.

One elevated blood pressure doesn't mean you have high blood pressure, but it does mean you need to have your blood pressure checked regularly. If the average of two or more diastolic blood pressure readings is 90 mm Hg or greater, or if the average of two or more systolic blood pressure readings is 140 mm Hg or greater, you have high blood pressure.

The following blood pressures are considered acceptable for adolescents and children:

Age	Blood pressure should be:
18 or older	less than 140/90
14 to 18 years	less than 135/90
10 to 14 years	less than 125/85
6 to 10 years	less than 120/80
less than 6 years	less than 110/75

For adults, the following blood pressure readings are used to determine if your high blood pressure is mild, moderate, or severe:

Defining Hypertension

DIASTOLIC Blood Pressure (mm Hg)	SYSTOLIC Blood Pressure (mm Hg)		
	less than 140	140 to 159	160 or greater
less than 85	normal blood pressure	borderline systolic hypertension	systolic hypertension
85 to 89	high normal blood pressure		
90 to 104	————	mild hypertension	————
105 to 114	————	moderate hypertension	————
115 or greater	————	severe hypertension	————

Source: 1984 Report of the Joint National Committee on Detection, Evaluation, and Treatment of High Blood Pressure.

Some people have a form of hypertension in which blood pressure occasionally rises above 140/90 mm Hg. This type of high blood pressure may seem to come and go, but it still can be serious.

The general consensus is the lower the blood pressure the better. However, if you find yourself getting dizzy when you stand up quickly, you may have hypotension, or low blood pressure.

What causes hypertension?

There are two categories of hypertension. The first type is "essential" or "primary" hypertension, the cause of which is unknown. Most cases of hypertension fall into this first category. The other type is called "secondary" hypertension, which means it is the result of some known cause. The main causes of secondary hypertension are problems with kidneys, blood vessels, or hormonal imbalance. Whether you have primary or secondary hypertension, you should attempt to control it as soon as it's discovered.

Although the cause of hypertension is often unknown, various factors seem to raise blood pressure: body weight, heredity, sodium intake, kidney function, action of some body hormones, medications, lifestyle habits, and dietary factors besides sodium. Let's look at each risk factor more closely.

Obesity

An increase in body weight or fat usually is followed by an increase in blood pressure. Obesity seems to strain the circulatory system, which can cause an increase in blood pressure. Losing weight has been shown to lower blood pressure in many overweight persons. If you are overweight and have high blood pressure, weight loss should be your first step in treating it.

Heredity

Heredity can have a strong influence on your blood pressure. Researchers estimate between 15 to 20 percent of all Americans have inherited the genes that make them prone to high blood pressure. Unfortunately, there's no way to determine who has inherited these genes. None of us knows for sure what our genes "have in store" for us. Family history is the only guide.

However, we do know that blacks (Afro-Americans) have a higher incidence of hypertension than people of other races. They also tend to be more prone to organ damage (stroke, heart problems, kidney problems) from high blood pressure.

Sodium Intake

Many studies have linked high levels of sodium intake to an increase in blood pressure. Populations with large amounts of sodium in their diets, such as the Northern Japanese, have high rates of hypertension and death from stroke.

Heredity seems to play a critical role in how sensitive you are to sodium. As mentioned, some individuals seem to be susceptible to high blood pressure. For these people, high amounts of sodium in the diet can cause problems. Since we can't determine who is and who isn't sensitive to sodium, it's a good idea for all of us to limit our sodium intake.

Fluid Balance

The role of sodium and potassium in hypertension is difficult to understand. They're the two minerals involved in the regulation of body fluids and blood pressure.

Most of the sodium in your body (95 percent) is in the fluid that surrounds the body cells. Only a small amount of sodium is actually inside the cells.

Sodium regulates the amount of water or body fluids in the bloodstream. Sodium and water volume are carefully balanced by the ability of the kidneys to get rid of excess sodium. Abnormal levels of sodium in the blood can affect the nerves, muscles, and normal thought process (people often become confused), as well as blood pressure.

Potassium is the main mineral found within the cells; 80 percent is inside the cells and 20 percent is in the bloodstream. Potassium has many important functions. It activates enzymes necessary for processing and storing carbohydrates. It helps send nerve messages to the heart and skeletal muscles. Abnormal potassium levels—either too high or low—can lead to muscle weakness or irregular heart beats.

The body works continuously to move sodium out of the cells and potassium into the cells. However, too much sodium in the fluid around the cells upsets the balance and fluid accumulates. This extra fluid puts pressure on the outside of the blood vessels, making it harder for the heart to pump blood through them.

Sodium may not be the only or even the actual cause of hypertension, but too much sodium can aggravate the situation.

Kidney Function

The kidneys play a major role in regulating blood pressure. They get rid of excess sodium and water and regulate sodium and potassium balance. If the kidneys can't clear away the sodium, the blood volume goes up. The heart then has to work harder, and blood pressure rises.

Hormones and Stress

Two hormones produced by the adrenal gland, epinephrine and norepinephrine, stimulate the heart to pump faster and the small arteries to constrict. This also raises the blood pressure. Since these hormones often are produced by the body during stress, long periods of stress might be a factor in hypertension.

Two other hormones also can increase blood pressure. They are renin, made in the kidney, and aldosterone, made in the adrenal gland. For some as yet unknown reason, some people produce too much of these hormones.

Lifestyle Habits

Smoking causes a narrowing of the blood vessels, which forces the heart to work harder. Smoking definitely puts you at greater risk for hypertension.

People who drink large amounts of alcohol also tend to have high blood pressure. If you smoke and drink, you're putting yourself at even greater risk.

High fat, high cholesterol diet

Simply put, fat and cholesterol clog up arteries. This is referred to as atherosclerosis or hardening of the arteries. As fatty deposits build up on the blood vessels, the blood pressure has to go up to push blood through the narrowed vessels. Narrowing of the blood vessels and the arteries that supply the heart is the usual cause of heart attacks.

Medications

A number of medications can raise blood pressure or interfere with the effectiveness of drugs used to treat hypertension. These include birth control pills (oral contraceptives), steroids, nasal decongestants, appetite suppressants, and some antidepressants. When you're buying medications, or if you're wondering about something you already use, it's smart to ask your pharmacist about it. Also, be sure your doctor knows what medications you're taking.

Minerals

Calcium, potassium, and chloride may also play a role in hypertension. But at the moment, we don't know why or how they're involved. No doubt, we'll be hearing more about these minerals in the future.

What should you do if you have hypertension?

The National High Blood Pressure Program of the National Heart, Lung, and Blood Institute recommends the following to reduce high blood pressure:

1. Lose weight. This should be the first step for people who are more than 20 pounds over their desirable body weight or have a high percentage of body fat. Weight loss often results in a substantial drop in blood pressure.

2. Limit daily sodium. Reducing the amount of sodium you use each day to about 2,000 to 3,000 milligrams will help lower your blood pressure. Part II of this book will help you reduce the amount of sodium in your diet.

3. If you drink alcohol, do so in moderation. Try not to drink more than 2 ounces of alcohol per day (2 ounces of liquor, 8 ounces of wine, or 24 ounces of beer).

4. Reduce your intake of saturated fats. Replace them with unsaturated fats and complex carbohydrates with fiber.

5. Don't smoke. People who smoke increase their risk for coronary heart and blood vessel disease.

6. Get regular aerobic exercise. It improves fitness, reduces body fat, helps control weight, and is a good way to relieve stress.

Aerobic means "with oxygen." Aerobic exercises are those you can do for a long time without shortness of breath. This type of exercise uses many muscles and strengthens the heart and

lungs. Brisk walking, cycling, swimming, jogging, skating, and cross-country skiing are excellent aerobic exercises.

Activities such as sprinting up a hill or running up a flight of stairs are hard on the heart and lungs. You can quickly become exhausted when doing this type of exercise. We call these anaerobic exercises because the body runs out of oxygen. (Anaerobic means "without oxygen.")

Certain types of anaerobic exercise, such as strenuous weight lifting, may increase blood pressure to dangerous levels, especially if you already have hypertension. Be sure to exercise, but do so with caution.

7. Learn to do things that are relaxing or restful for you. Stress can aggravate high blood pressure.

In addition to these recommendations, other important suggestions for controlling high blood pressure include:

8. Follow medical advice in taking prescribed blood pressure medicine. Doctors prescribe several types of medications to control blood pressure:
— Diuretics promote excretion of water and sodium, which reduces the volume of blood and lowers blood pressure.
— Some drugs block the sympathetic nervous system. The most commonly used are called beta blockers. They relax blood vessels and decrease the heart rate by blocking nerve impulses in the heart and blood vessels. The slower heart rate means less work for the heart. Adrenergic-inhibiting agents work in much the same way as beta blockers.
— Vasodilators relax and open up blocked vessels, including small arteries.
— Calcium channel blockers prevent calcium from constricting blood vessels.
— Angiotension-Coverting-Enzyme (ACE) inhibitors slow the production of some hormones that constrict blood vessels.

The type of medication you use will vary, depending on certain other health problems—for example, diabetes.

9. Increase the amount of fiber in your diet. According to some researchers, people who eat fiber-rich diets have lower blood pressure than those who don't. A diet high in fiber not only reduces blood cholesterol levels, but it may also reduce diastolic blood pressure.

Some Common Heart and Blood Pressure Medications

Type	Generic names	Brand names
BLOOD PRESSURE DIURETICS Thiazide type	hydrochlorothiazide chlorothiazide	HydroDIURIL Diuril
Potassium- sparing	spironolactone triamterene amiloride	Aldactone Dyrenium Midamor
Others	furosemide metholazone bumetanide chlorthalidone	Lasix Diulo, Zaroxolyn, Bumex Hygroton
BETA BLOCKERS Nonspecific	propranolol nadolol pindolol	Inderal Corgard Visken
Specific	atenolol metoprolol	Tenormin Lopressor
BLOOD VESSEL DILATORS (VASODILATORS)	prazosin hydralazine minoxidil clonidine guanabenz methyldopa captopril enalapril	Minipress Apresoline Loniten Catapres Wytensin Aldomet Capoten Vasotec
OTHERS	reserpine guanethidine indapamide	(several combination products) Ismelin, Esimil Lozol
CALCIUM CHANNEL BLOCKERS	nifedipine verapamil diltiazem	Procardia Calan, Isoptin Cardizem

Adapted from "Heart and Blood Pressure Medications: How They Work and What They Do" by Greg Mills, Pharm. D., Diabetes Self-Management, Sept/Oct 1987.

10. Avoid caffeine. Just two or three cups of coffee each day can raise both the systolic and the diastolic pressures an average of 10 mm Hg or more. This increase may last up to three hours.

11. Have your blood pressure checked regularly. Remember, high blood pressure often has no symptoms.

12. When buying over-the-counter drugs, look at the ingredient list and warning statement on the label to see if sodium has been added. Some drugs contain large amounts of sodium.

Many over-the-counter antacid preparations have high levels of sodium in the form of sodium bicarbonate, sodium citrate, and sodium phosphate. A statement of sodium content must appear on labels of antacids with 5 milligrams or more of sodium per dose (tablet, teaspoon, etc.). If you do use antacids, look for those based on magnesium hydroxide, aluminum hydroxide, or calcium carbonate.

Some laxatives also contain large amounts of sodium in the form of sodium bicarbonate, sodium phosphate, and sodium citrate. Sleeping aids that contain sodium citrate are another source of sodium.

Other over-the-counter medicines don't have sodium but do have other ingredients that raise blood pressure. Cold, allergy, and diet medications containing phenylpropanolamine (PPA) raise blood pressure. Many pain killers, diuretics, and stimulants have caffeine, which increases blood pressure.

Some companies are now producing low-sodium over-the-counter products. If in doubt, ask your pharmacist about the drug and if it is appropriate for you to use.

13. Here's a little-known fact you might appreciate. People who have hypertension should go easy on black licorice, especially if they take diuretics. It can make the body retain sodium and lose potassium in the urine. It also causes fluid retention. Incidentally, chewing tobacco contains licorice.

Spice for Life

Part II

Choosing Foods Wisely

Limiting your sodium intake is one of the first steps in treating hypertension, and helping you do just that is one of the main goals of this book. In this section, you will find specific guidelines about how much sodium you should use and how to make wise food choices that are low in sodium but still allow you to enjoy your food.

Salt and sodium: Is there a difference?

When we hear the terms "salt" or "sodium," we usually think of table salt. Actually, as we said earlier, table salt is composed of two chemicals—sodium and chloride. About one-third of the sodium in our diets comes straight from the salt shaker. So cutting down on table salt is a good way to cut down on sodium. But what about the other two-thirds? Much of that comes from processed foods.

Sodium added to foods comes in many forms. Besides sodium chloride (salt), the most common forms are monosodium glutamate (MSG), sodium bicarbonate (baking soda), sodium nitrite or nitrate (meat preservatives), baking powder, disodium phosphate, sodium alginate, sodium benzoate, sodium hydroxide, sodium propionate, sodium sulfite, and sodium saccharin (sweetener). Sometimes, as in the case of sodium saccharin, the actual amount of sodium will be small. In other products, especially when there are several sodium compounds, the amount of sodium will be significant.

Sodium also occurs naturally in food and in some drinking water. Also, if you use a water softener, you are adding unnecessary sodium to your diet. Since there's not much we can do to reduce natural sodium, we need to concentrate on avoiding high-sodium foods and finding different ways to flavor food.

How much sodium do we need?

Although some sodium is necessary for the body to function, we consume far more than we need. The body requires only about 220 milligrams of sodium per day, or the equivalent of 1/10 teaspoon of salt. (One teaspoon of salt contains 2,300 milligrams of sodium.) Yet the average intake in the U.S. and Canada is 4,000 to 5,000 milligrams of sodium—or 2 to 3 teaspoons of salt—per day. We could easily get all the sodium we need even if we never added salt in processing or cooking food.

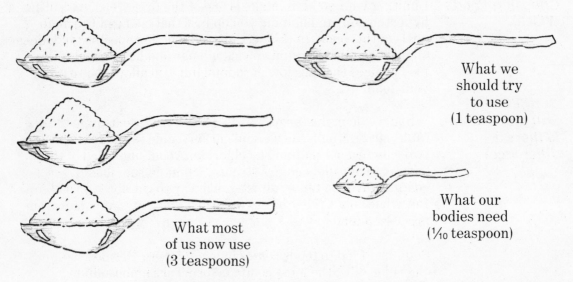

What we
should try
to use
(1 teaspoon)

What our
bodies need
(1/10 teaspoon)

What most
of us now use
(3 teaspoons)

The American Heart Association recommends we use no more than 3,000 milligrams of sodium per day — or about 1 teaspoon of salt. Some people should use even less. Your doctor or dietitian can help you decide what is best for you.

High blood pressure isn't the only reason we should watch our salt intake. A low-sodium diet also is important for controlling swelling (edema), heart and circulation problems, fluid build-up in the abdomen (ascites) caused by cirrhosis of the liver, and the side effects of some prescribed medications, such as corticosteroids.

How to break the sodium habit

Adding salt to our food is a habit we can change. Our desire for salt is an acquired taste, not one we are born with. When you first begin to eliminate salt, food may seem less tasty. After three to six weeks, though, your taste buds will adjust. Then you'll be amazed to discover some new flavors! The following tips can help you get started:

1. Stop adding salt to foods at the table. Remove the salt shaker. Pass the Pepper!
2. Taste food before deciding if it really needs salt. Try using less salt, or use seasonings and spices to flavor your food.

3. Cut back or eliminate salt in cooking and baking.

4. Learn to choose foods low in sodium—at home and when dining out.

5. Read labels to learn the sodium content of foods. Use low-sodium products.

How much sodium should you consume?

Everyone has individual needs. Your doctor or dietitian can help you determine what health problems you have and how much sodium you should be using.

Here's what you might expect with various medical risks. These recommendations are based on a well-balanced diet containing a minimum of four servings of starch/bread, five to six ounces of meat or meat substitute, two servings of vegetables, two servings of fruit, and two servings of milk per day.

Recommended Sodium Intake

Health Factors	Sodium Level	Dietary Guidelines
Healthy person who wants to control sodium intake for disease prevention.	3000 milligrams per day	1) Eliminate use of table salt. 2) Seldom use foods with more than 800 milligrams of sodium per serving.
Mild hypertension Mild heart disease Mild fluid retention	2000 milligrams per day	1) Eliminate use of table salt; use minimal amounts of salt in cooking. 2) Avoid foods containing more than 400 milligrams of sodium per serving.
Moderate to severe hypertension Kidney disease Heart disease Moderate to severe fluid retention	1000-2000 milligrams per day	1) Eliminate use of table salt; use minimal amounts of salt in cooking. 2) Eat only foods with less than 140 milligrams of sodium per serving.

How to make low-sodium food choices.

The following pages list the sodium content of many common foods. The foods are grouped into these categories:

Starch/Bread
Meat (with an additional section on
    convenience and fast foods used
    as a main course)
Vegetable
Fruit
Milk
Fat
Condiments

Each list shows four levels of sodium to make it easier for you to decide which foods to use. Once you have decided how much sodium you should use each day (see Recommended Sodium Intake, p. 27), you can use that information to decide whether you can occasionally eat high-sodium foods or whether you should stick with only low-sodium foods.

***Special tips on
using these lists***

- The number in parentheses after each food item is the approximate amount of sodium in milligrams per serving. For example, if you want to know how much sodium is in oyster crackers, you will find the following listing: oyster crackers, 24, (200). This tells you 24 oyster crackers have 200 milligrams of sodium.

- The sodium content is for the portion listed. If you eat a larger portion, you will naturally consume more sodium. It helps to measure portion sizes until you are able to "eyeball" the correct amount.

- An asterisk (*) means the sodium level is for food as prepared according to package directions, many of which call for salt added to the cooking water or during the cooking process. You can usually omit the salt called for in cooking without sacrificing the taste.

- Unless specified, our figures are not for any particular brand name item. Sodium values do vary. Different brands may have different amounts of sodium. It's best to check the label.

- As a general rule, fresh is best. A great deal of sodium is added during processing.

Important note: Sodium values will vary a great deal from product to product. Please remember the values listed in the tables are approximate.

STARCH/BREAD:

Many foods are found in the carbohydrate category. Therefore, we have divided them into groups for easier reference: breads, cereals, soups, crackers and snacks, gravies, and desserts. Since many foods in this section are processed, the sodium content can be high. Read the label.

SODIUM	0-140 mg.

BREADS

bread sticks, 4″ long, 2 (140)
corn tortilla, 1 (53)
diet bread, 1 slice (115)
dinner roll, 1 (140)
raisin bread, 1 slice (102)
rice cake, 2 (20)
salt-free bread, 1 slice (0)
thin-slice bread, 1 slice (80)
white bread, 1 slice (140)
whole wheat bread,
   1 slice (140)
yeast doughnut, 1 (100)

CEREALS

cooked cereal, reg. or quick,
   ½ cup (1-5)
granola, 1 oz. (90)
puffed rice or wheat,
   1½ cups (0)
Miller's Bran,
   2 Tbsp. (0)
shredded wheat, ½ cup (2)
wheat germ, 2 Tbsp. (0)

SOUPS

commercial low-sodium
   soups, 1 cup (25-50)

140-400 mg.	400-800 mg.	800 + mg.

bagel, 1 (198)
baking powder biscuit,
    1 (275)
bread cubes, seasoned,
    1 cup (391)
bread cubes, unseasoned,
    1 cup (207)
cake doughnut, 1 (160)
croissant, 1 (230)
English muffin, 1 (360)
French bread, 3″ slice (162)
French toast, 1 slice (185)
frozen pastry, 1 (120-200)
hamburger/hot dog bun,
    1 (292)
muffin, 1½″ high (175)
pancake, 2 (304)
pumpernickle, 1 slice (159)
refrigerator roll, 1 (340)
rye bread, 1 slice (156)
taco shell, 2 (145)
waffle, 1 square (345)

bran cereal, ½ cup (175-300)
cooked cereal,* ½ cup (200-300)
Grape-Nuts, 3 Tbsp. (150)
instant hot cereal, 1 packet
    (260-360)
ready-to-eat unsweetened
    cereals, ¾ cup (170-390)

commercial reduced-sodium
    soups, 1 cup (175-250)

bread crumbs, unseasoned,
    ⅔ cup (491)
corn bread, 1, 2½″
    square (491)
hoagie roll, 1 (782)
stuffing mix,* ½ cup (650)
Vienna-type breadstick,
    1 (548)

bread crumbs, seasoned,
    ⅔ cup (1411)

bean soup, 1 cup (1000-1200)
bouillon, 1 cup (1440)
bouillon cube, 1 (966)
Chunky Soup,
    1 cup (1100-1400)
cream soup, 1 cup (1000)
vegetable or broth, 1 cup
    (800-1100)

SODIUM	0-140 mg.

CRACKERS AND SNACKS

animal crackers, 8 (65)
French fries, unsalted, 10 (15)
graham crackers, 3 (140)
large kernel popcorn no salt
    added, 3 cups (trace)
low-salt crackers, 1 oz.
    (90-120)
matzo, unsalted, 6″ (135)
melba toast, 5 (15)
pretzels, unsalted, 1 oz. (5)
salt-free potato chips, 1 oz. (4)
Wasa bröd, 2 (130)

GRAINS

all purpose flour, 2½ Tbsp. (0)
bulgur, 2 Tbsp. (1)
corn meal, 2½ Tbsp. (0)
grits, ½ cup (0)
pasta, ½ cup (1)
rice, ⅓ cup (0)

DESSERTS AND SWEETS

These foods may be high
in sugar and saturated fats.

brownie, 3″ (70)
chocolate bar, 1.65 oz. (45)
cookies, 2 medium (100)
diet gelatin, ½ cup (60)
frozen yogurt, ½ cup (115)
gelatin, ½ cup (50-90)
gingersnaps, 3 (120)
ice cream, ½ cup (60)
granola bar, 1 (85-150)
popsicle, 1 (10)
sherbet, ½ cup (22)
vanilla wafers, 6 (50)

140-400 mg.	400-800 mg.	800 + mg.

butter-type crackers,
   4-6 (180-220)
corn chips, 1 oz. (180 or more)
microwave popcorn, 4 cups
   (310-440)
oyster crackers, 24 (200)
potato chips, 1 oz.
   (140 or more)
RyKrisp crackers,
   unseasoned, 4 (229)
saltines, 6 (187)
whole wheat crackers, 5 (150)

cheese puffs, 1 oz.
   (370 or more)
pretzels, 1 oz. (400-700)

Bisquick, ¼ cup (350)
chow mein noodles
   ½ cup (205)
grits,* ½ cup (270)
rice,* ⅓ cup (183)

pasta side dish, packaged,*
   ½ cup (500-700)

angel food cake,
   1/10 (140-275)
cake, 1/12 (190-400)
double crust pie, 1/6 pie (400)
malted milk shake,
   10 oz. (300)
milk shake, 10 oz. (210)
pudding, ½ cup (230)
Snickers candy bar, 1 (170)

Boston cream pie, ⅛ (405)
cream pie, ⅛ (380-500)
sugar free pudding,
   ½ cup (420)

MEATS AND MEAT SUBSTITUTES:

Meats and main dishes can contain excessive amounts of sodium. A good rule of thumb for avoiding too much sodium is to purchase fresh meats rather than processed meats and main dishes. Most of the sodium amounts listed below are per a 1-ounce serving, but you should be aware that 3 ounces or more is an average serving size.

SODIUM	0-140 mg.

MEATS AND CHEESE

bacon, 1 slice (101)
beef, pork, lamb, poultry, wild game & duck, fresh, 1 oz. (15-20)
beef, pork, lamb, poultry, fresh, 3 oz. (75)
cream cheese, 1 oz. (41)
egg, 1 (69)
egg substitute, ¼ cup (90)
farmers cheese, 1 oz. (135)
fish, 1 oz. (20-40)
lobster, 2 oz. (120)
mozzarella, 1 oz. (132)
organ meats—liver, kidney, 1 oz. (15-75)
peanut butter, 1 Tbsp. (75)
ricotta, 1 oz. (35)
salt-free canned tuna 1 oz. (10)
shelled salted nuts, 1 oz. (100)
shrimp, 2 oz. (80)
Swiss, 1 oz. (74)

140-400 mg.	400-800 mg.	800 + mg.

boiled ham (sandwich type),
  1 oz. (373)
canned salmon, ¼ cup (213)
cheddar cheese, 1 oz. (176)
corned beef, 1 oz. (267)
cottage cheese, ¼ cup (230)
grated Parmesan cheese
  2 Tbsp., (186)
Gouda cheese, 1 oz. (235)
ground pork sausage,
  1 oz. (369)
ham, canned, 1 oz. (267)
ham, cured, 1 oz. (376)
Havarti, 1 oz. (200)
Monterey Jack, 1 oz. (152)
processed cheese,
  1 oz. (275-445)
Provolone, 1 oz. (250)
sardines, 2 med. (198)
sausage, 1 oz. (250-450)
scallops, 2 oz. (152)
turkey bologna, 1 oz. (230)
turkey pastrami, 1 oz. (280)

American cheese, 1 oz. (420)
beef and pork frankfurter,
  1 (510)
blue cheese, 1 oz. (396)
Canadian bacon, 1 oz. (440)
canned crab, 2 oz. (570)
canned tuna, ¼ cup (403)
cheese spread, 1 oz. (400-625)
chicken frankfurter,
  1 oz. (620)
low-cholesterol or low-
  calorie cheese,
  1 oz. (350-450)
luncheon meat, 1 oz. (300-400)
nacho cheese sauce,
  ¼ cup (596)
sardines, 8 (510)
turkey frank, 1 (642)

bratwurst, 3 oz. (820)
dried beef, 1 oz. (1220)
ham, canned, 3 oz. (801)
ham, cured, 3 oz. (1128)
smoked herring, 1 oz. (1744)

VEGETABLES:

Most fresh vegetables, like most fruits, are naturally low in sodium; however, a few exceptions exist. Unless a very restricted sodium diet is prescribed, all fresh vegetables can be used. Canning can add a considerable amount of sodium, so read the label.

SODIUM	0-140 mg.

artichoke, ½ med. (40)
corn on the cob, 1 ear (13)
fresh/frozen beets, carrots, celery, ½ cup (40-55)
frozen greens, ½ cup (40-80)
vegetables, fresh/frozen, ½ cup (1-25)

STARCHY VEGE-TABLES

dried beans, peas, lentils, cooked, ½ cup (0-13)
fresh or canned sweet potato ⅓ cup (36)
fresh peas and squash, ¾ cup (4-7)
frozen peas, lima beans, ½ cup (50-90)
frozen potato products, ½ cup (30-60)
potato, 1 (7)
yams, pumpkin, ⅓ cup (4)

140-400 mg.	400-800 mg.	800 + mg.

beet greens, cooked,
 ½ cup (175)
canned vegetables,
 ½ cup (170-500)

canned sauerkraut,
 ½ cup (780)
canned tomato sauce,
 ½ cup (610-760)
tomato juice, ½ cup (445)
vegetable juice, ½ cup (445)

baked beans, canned,
 ¼ cup (216)
canned corn, ½ cup (286)
canned lima beans,
 ½ cup (309)
canned peas, ½ cup (186)
potatoes, instant,*
 ½ cup (360)

au gratin potato, packaged,*
 ½ cup (630)
canned kidney beans,
 ½ cup (420)
hash browns packaged,*
 ½ cup (460)
scalloped potatoes,*
 ½ cup (570)
spaghetti or pizza sauce,
 ½ cup (600-800)

potato salad, ½ cup (920)

FRUITS:

Fruits are naturally very low in sodium. Canning, freezing, or drying generally adds very little sodium.

SODIUM	0-140 mg.

FRUITS
canned fruits (5-15)
dried apples, 4 rings (23)
dried fruits (1-25)
fresh fruits (2-15)
frozen fruits (10)
juices—frozen, fresh or
  canned (5)
melon, ⅓ (16)

DAIRY:

Milk naturally has sodium. Because it is an excellent source of protein, calcium and vitamin D, 2 cups per day is recommended regardless of sodium restriction.

SODIUM	0-140 mg.

DAIRY
hot cocoa, 1 cup (128)
powdered milk, ⅓ cup (126)
skim, 1%, 2%, and whole milk,
  1 cup (120-130)

BEVERAGES:

Nearly all drinking water has some sodium. The amount varies, but it is usually small in most water supplies. Except for some individuals on strict low-sodium diets, the amount of sodium that water adds is not significant. However, do not drink water that has been softened. Check with local city offices regarding sodium content of city water.

SODIUM	0-140 mg.

BEVERAGES
beer, 12 oz. (25)
club soda, 12 oz. (75)
coffee, tea, limeade,
  Kool-Aid, fruit drink (2-5)
diet soft drink, with
  NutraSweet or saccharin,
  12 oz. (0-100)
distilled liquor, 1 oz. (1)
lemonade, 8 oz. (50)
mineral water, 8 oz. (40)
regular soft drink, 12 oz. (70)
wine, 4 oz. (12)

140-400 mg.	400-800 mg.	800 + mg.
NONE	NONE	NONE

140-400 mg.	400-800 mg.	800 + mg.

condensed milk, ½ cup (160)
eggnog, ½ cup (160)
evaporated skim milk,
  ½ cup (147)
low-fat buttermilk, 1 cup
  (260)
low-fat plain or fruited
  yogurt, 1 cup (131-250)		

140-400 mg.	400-800 mg.	800 + mg.
Gatorade, 8 oz. (140)		

FATS:

This category includes foods high in fat content. Be careful how much of these products you use. Generally, 1 tablespoon per day is premissible.

SODIUM	0-140 mg.

FATS	bacon, 1 slice (100)
	butter, 1 tsp. (40)
	dry cream substitute,
	   2 Tbsp. (25)
	lard, 1 Tbsp. (0)
	margarine, 1 tsp. (50)
	mayonnaise, 1 Tbsp. (80)
	mission olives, 3 ripe (100)
	oil, 1 tsp. (0)
	reduced-calorie margarine
	   1 Tbsp. (110)
	reduced-calorie mayonnaise,
	   1 Tbsp. (88)
	salad dressing,
	   1 Tbsp. (100-140)
	salad dressing
	   (Miracle Whip), 1 tsp. (70)
	shortening, 1 tsp. (0)
	sour cream, 2 Tbsp. (12)
	unsalted butter or margarine,
	   1 tsp. (1)
	unsalted nuts, 1/3 oz. (1)

CONDIMENTS, ETC:

Condiments add the majority of sodium in processed and prepared foods. Instead of seasoning foods with salts, try herbs and spices.

SODIUM	0-140 mg.
CONDI-MENTS, ETC.	chili powder, 1 tsp. (26) cooking wine, 1/4 cup (138) garlic powder, 1 tsp. (1) gelatin, 1/2 cup (0) lemon juice, 1 Tbsp. (3) onion powder, 1 tsp. (1) pepper, 1 tsp. (1) prepared mustard, 1 tsp. (65) sugar free jelly, 2 tsp. (20) Tabasco sauce, 1 tsp. (24) vinegar, 1/2 cup (1) Worcestershire sauce 1 tsp. (49)

140-400 mg.	400-800 mg.	800 + mg.

French dressing,
  1 Tbsp. (220)
green olives, 4 (325)
nuts, ¼ cup (200-300)
ripe olives, 10 med. (280)
salad dressing, 1 Tbsp. (143)

reduced-calorie dressing,
  2 Tbsp. (450)

140-400 mg.	400-800 mg.	800 + mg.

A-1 sauce, 1 Tbsp. (275)
bacon bits, 1 Tbsp. (230)
barbecue sauce, 1 Tbsp. (230)
catsup, 1 Tbsp. (145)
chili sauce, 1 Tbsp. (227)
chip dip, 2 Tbsp.
  (130-255)
horse radish, 1 tsp. (230)
Worchestershire sauce,
  1 Tbsp. (150)

baking powder, 1 tsp. (340)
low sodium soy sauce,
  1 Tbsp. (600)
MSG, 1 tsp. (500)
packaged gravey mix,*
  ½ cup (500-1100)
salsa sauce, ¼ cup (385-590)
teriyaki sauce, 1 Tbsp. (690)

baking soda, 1 tsp. (821)
dill pickle, 1 med. (928)
garlic salt, 1 tsp. (1850)
lite salt, 1 Tbsp. (1196)
meat tenderizer, 1 tsp. (1750)
onion salt, 1 tsp. (1620)
salt, 1 tsp. (1940)
soy sauce, 1 tsp. (1029)

CONVENIENCE AND FAST FOODS

When using convenience and fast foods, remember the sodium content is based on the entire product rather than each individual component. For example, a hamburger consists of one bun, providing 230 milligrams sodium, and a 3-ounce hamburger unsalted, providing 75 milligrams, for a total of 405 milligrams.

A quick rule of thumb for use of these foods is to limit your sodium intake at one meal to ⅓ of your daily sodium allotment.

Remember, condiments will add more sodium; eliminate or use sparingly.

This list shows convenience and fast foods listed from the lowest in sodium to the highest. A few homemade items are included for comparison.

frozen fish fillet, 3 oz. (300-500)
taco, 1 (400)
fast food hamburger, 1 (500)
homemade lasagna, 1 serving (475)
chow mein,* 1 cup (500)
low cal. frozen dinner, 1 (500-1300)
pot pie, homemade, 1 (650)
cheese pizza (frozen, commercial,
    homemade), ¼ of 10% % pie, (650-730)
beef and macaroni,* frozen, 6 oz. (675)
fast food quarter pounder (700)
homemade chow mein, 1 cup (720)
chef salad with 1 Tbsp. dressing, 1 (800)
pot pie, frozen, 1 (800-1000)
macaroni and cheese,* 1 cup (800-1185)
canned chili, 1 cup (800-2000)
frozen Mexican entree, 1 (800-2550)
canned or homemade spaghetti,
    1 cup (850-1100)
fast food fish burger, 1 (880)

packaged noodle dinner, 1 serving
    (900-1100)
frozen meat (fish or chicken) dinner,
    1 (900-1400)
taco salad, 1 (925)
Reuben sandwich, 1 (925)
fast food jumbo hamburger, 1 (990)
canned beef and macaroni, 1 cup
    (1000-1250)
homemade macaroni and cheese, 1 cup
    (1090)
sausage/pepperoni pizza, ¼ of 13% % pie
    (1100-1500)
corn dog, 1 (1250)
canned Spanish rice, 1 cup (1370)
canned hash, 1 cup (1500)
frozen chow mein, 12 oz. (2300)
fast food chicken dinner, 1 (2245)
large size frozen dinner, 1 (3500-3800)

Read the label for sodium truth!

About half our daily sodium comes from sodium compounds added during processing. You'll find salt or sodium in almost all processed foods. It's important to read the label to know how much a product contains.

The Food and Drug Administration (FDA) developed the following guidelines to make sodium labeling less confusing:

Sodium free: less than 5 milligrams of sodium per serving.

Very low sodium: 35 milligrams or less of sodium per serving.

Low sodium: 140 milligrams or less of sodium per serving.

Reduced sodium: the sodium content has been reduced by at least 75 percent. In this instance, the food label must show the sodium content of both the normal product and the reduced-sodium product.

Unsalted, no salt added, without added salt: These terms can be used only if no salt has been added to a product normally processed with salt.

In addition, foods making any of the above claims must list on the label the milligrams of sodium per serving.

Some ingredients to beware of:

Common food additives

anhydrous disodium phosphate
brine
calcium disodium
dioctyl sodium sulfosuccinate
disodium dihydrogen pyrophosphate
disodium guanylate
disodium inosinate
disodium phosphate
monosodium glutamate
salt pork
sea salt
sodium acid pyrophosphate
sodium alginate
sodium aluminosilicate
sodium aluminum
sodium ascorbate
sodium benzoate
sodium biphosphate
sodium bisulfite
sodium carboxymethyl cellulose
sodium caseinate

sodium chloride
sodium citrate
sodium erythorbate
sodium ferrocyanide
sodium gluconate
sodium hexametaphosphate
sodium hydroxide
sodium iron pyrophosphate
sodium metaphosphate
sodium nitrate
sodium nitrite
sodium preservatives
sodium propionate
sodium phosphate
sodium saccharin
sodium stearoly-2-lactylate
sodium thiosulfate
sodium triosulfate
sodium tripolyphosphate
trisodium citrate

Cooking ingredients

baking powder
baking soda
celery salt

flour (self-rising)
garlic salt
onion salt

The list of ingredients on the label will also tell you about the sodium content of the food. Ingredients are listed in descending order. In other words, if salt or some other sodium-containing ingredient appears at the top of the list, the product is probably not for you.

For more specific information on sodium content, look for the nutrition information per serving. This information is not required on all labels, but it is required for foods making specific nutritional claims. Many manufacturers voluntarily put this information on their labels. In this case, the label must tell you the milligrams of sodium per serving.

As of 1986, the milligrams of sodium in the serving size is required on products with nutrition labeling.

The amount of food for which nutrition information is given and the number of servings in the container.

**Nutrition Information
Per Serving**

Serving size. . . . . 1 oz
Servings per container. . . 6
Calories. 130
Protein. . . . . 3 g
Carbohydrate. . . . . . . 18 g
Fat. . . . . 7 g
Sodium. . . . . 190 mg

**Percentage of
U.S. Recommended Daily
Allowances (U.S. RDA)**

Protein. 6
Vitamin A. . . . . *
Vitamin C. 2
Thiamin. 6
Riboflavin. . . . . *
Niacin. 4
Calcium. . . . . *
Iron. 6

*Contains less than 2% of the U.S. RDA for these nutrients

If you use a particular food that doesn't include nutrition information, you might try writing to the manufacturer to request the information. Even better, ask them to include it on their label. Most companies are willing to give out nutrition information if you ask for it.

Dining out?

Restaurants pose a difficult challenge. But that doesn't mean you should give up eating out. Many restaurants will gladly cook your meal to fit your special needs. Knowing what to avoid and what to choose will help make dining out the pleasure it should be.

The "menu" below provides some suggestions.

Appetizers

- Try a raw vegetable platter with a small amount of dip.
- A fresh fruit compote or fruit juice is tasty and attractive.
- Raw oysters, clams, and shrimp are low in sodium; use just a small amount of sauce.
- Avoid chips, cheese, and pickled foods.
- If appropriate for your diet, a glass of wine, beer, or a cocktail is low in sodium.
- Avoid high-sodium mixers such as tomato juice and salted rims of margaritas.

Soups and Salads

Enjoy a salad with greens and raw vegetables. Ask for dressing on the side, and limit it to 1 tablespoon.

- Gelatin salads are usually low in sodium (but are high in sugar).
- Use vinegar and oil with freshly ground pepper or lemon juice instead of salad dressing.
- Avoid soup, even if it's homemade.
- Bacon, croutons, sunflower seeds, anchovies, and pickles are extremely high in sodium. Skip them or use sparingly.
- Carry your own low-sodium salad dressing or sodium-free seasoning.

Breads

- Most breads are not high in sodium, but it's best to stick with just one serving.
- Beware of crackers. Most are salty.

Entrees

- Choose fresh meat, poultry, or fish.

- Avoid heavily seasoned meats such as pastrami, corned beef, ham, canned meats or fish, and Canadian bacon.

- Ask the waiter if your entree can be prepared without added salt.

- Choose broiled, baked, or roasted meats.

- Skip breaded, marinated, or barbecued meats.

- If you use gravies and sauces, ask for them on the side; use 1 tablespoon only.

- Skip casserole-type dishes because sodium amounts can't be individualized. This includes items such as lasagna, spaghetti sauce, stew, or quiche.

- Cheese can add a lot of sodium; avoid cheese sauces and cheese dishes.

- Ask that Oriental dishes be prepared without salt, MSG, or soy sauce.

Sandwiches

- Fresh meats, poultry, or fish are the best choices.

- Lettuce, sprouts, raw onions, and tomato add crunchiness but no sodium.

- Use catsup and other sauces sparingly.

- Avoid salty meats such as pastrami, corned beef, ham, canned meat or fish, and Canadian bacon.
- Aged cheese has one-half the sodium of processed cheese.
- Avoid hot dogs, bratwurst, or Polish sausage.
- Peanut butter and jelly is a good low-sodium standby.
- Skip the pickle.
- A taco, burrito, or tostada without sauce is a low-sodium choice when eating Mexican food.

Vegetables

- Order fresh vegetables whenever possible.
- Ask for a lemon wedge to season vegetables.
- A baked potato is an excellent low-sodium choice. Don't add sodium by adding a lot of condiments.
- Ask for unsalted French fries.
- Carry your own salt substitutes or seasoning packets.

Desserts

- Fresh fruit is an excellent choice.
- A cookie, gelatin, or one scoop of ice cream or sherbet is a low-sodium choice.
- One slice of pound cake, sponge cake, or angel food cake is lower in sodium than most other desserts.

Breakfast Items

- Order eggs without salt added—poached, fried, or soft boiled.
- Avoid premade breakfast casseroles and items with added cheese, ham, or bacon—for example, quiche.
- Pancakes, muffins, English muffins, biscuits, and waffles are all prepared with salt.
- Choose hot cereal or a low-sodium dry cereal.
- Order fresh fruit or fruit juice; avoid vegetable juice.

Fast Foods

- Fast foods are often high is sodium. Many restaurants will tell you the sodium content if you ask.
- Some fast-food restaurants will try to meet special requests. Ask them to "hold the salt." Sauces are also a source of sodium; ask for them on the side or not at all.

• Condiments can add a lot sodium. The restaurant's nutrition information won't include the sodium content of condiments. So if you add ketchup, mustard, and relish to a hot dog, you're adding sodium.

• The sodium information provided by fast-food restaurants is based on the entire product rather than each individual component. For example, a hamburger consists of one bun, providing 230 milligrams of sodium, and a 3-ounce hamburger, providing 75 milligrams, for a total of 405 milligrams of sodium.

• A quick rule of thumb for fast-food dining is to limit your sodium intake at one meal to ⅓ of your total sodium for the day. For example, if your daily limit is 3,000 milligrams, ⅓ would be 1,000 milligrams. Try to keep the sodium level for one dinner within that limit. Using this simple gauge can help you judge whether your fast-food dinner has too much sodium.

Airline Meals

• Most airlines provide low-sodium meals with 24-hour advanced notice. Tell the flight attendent of your request when your board the flight.

Cooking the low-sodium way

Cooking without salt takes a little practice, just as choosing low sodium foods takes practice. Here are a few tips on ways to reduce the sodium in your cooking. You'll want to experiment to find the tastes you like best.

Eliminating salt

• The most obvious way to decrease sodium in cooking is simply NOT TO USE IT. For example, the cooking directions for many pastas, vegetables, and cereals call for adding salt to the cooking water.

You can easily skip the salt without losing much flavor. Many recipes call for more salt than necessary; you can use half the quantity called for and still have the same taste. In some recipes, you can leave the salt out altogether.

One caution about omitting salt in baking: Many recipes, especially those with yeast, require salt so the recipe will work. You may be able to reduce or even omit the salt used in baking, but the altered recipe may turn out differently than the original. Experiment to see what works.

• Rinsing foods also gets rid of sodium. A one-minute rinse of 6½ ounces of canned tuna will wash away about three-fourths of the sodium. Almost half of the sodium can be removed from canned vegetables by rinsing for one minute and heating the vegetables in tap water instead of the canning liquid.

Alternatives to salt and sodium in cooking

Aside from salt, many ingredients you use in the kitchen contain high levels of sodium. You'll want to avoid flavorings such as MSG, soy sauce, and garlic salt. Look for other ways to flavor food and retain the same good taste. Here are some of our favorite "tips."

• Onion and garlic powders are excellent alternatives to onion and garlic salts.

• Season stews, gravies, and soups with herbs, vinegar, or lemon juice instead of salt. Try adding a teaspoon of prepared mustard per cup of liquid or a few hearty dashes of angostura bitters.

• In place of soy sauce, steak sauce, and seasoned salt, use lemon juice or spices such as thyme, oregano, garlic, curry, cinnamon, chili powder, or tarragon.

• Vinegars flavored with fresh herbs add flavor and tang to low-sodium recipes. To make an herb vinegar, begin with 2 cups white, cider, or white wine vinegar and add 1 cup loosely packed fresh dill, oregano, chives, sage, basil, tarragon, or thyme. Let the mixture stand a few days, then strain. Pour it into a bottle and seal. This tastes wonderful on salads and vegetables.

• Citrus fruits are a low-sodium flavor alternative. Freshly grated peel can be added to sauces and dressings for some spark. Use lemon wedges at the table instead of salt.

• Many commerical low-sodium seasonings are available; some are excellent. For example:

lemon-pepper mixtures
salt-free steak sauce
salt-free ketchup
seasoned salt substitutes
all-purpose seasonings
herb seasonings
salad seasonings

Herbs and spices Herbs and spices are wonderful alternatives to salt and other products high in sodium. Many excellent commercial products are available including "all purpose seasonings" and herb seasonings. The American Heart Association has some excellent blends. Or try making these herb/spice blends yourself:

Saltless Surprise 2 tsp. garlic powder
1 tsp. basil
1 tsp. anise seed
1 tsp. oregano
1 tsp. powdered lemon rind or dry lemon juice

Put ingredients into blender and mix well. Store in glass container, label well, and add rice to prevent caking.

Herb Salt
Substitute

3 tsp. basil
2 tsp. savory (summer savory is best)
2 tsp. celery seed
2 tsp. ground cumin seed
2 tsp. sage
1 tsp. lemon thyme
2 tsp. marjoram

Mix well and then powder with mortar and pestle.

You can use virtually any herbs and spices in your kitchen.
The new tastes you discover will make your food much more
interesting. This table can guide you as you start experimenting.

HERB AND SPICE GUIDE FOR FOOD FLAVORING:

Herbs: the leaves, seeds or flowers of aromatic plants.
Fresh herbs are preferable. Dried herbs should not
be used in cold dishes. Use half as much of a dried herb
as you would a fresh one.

Spices: the roots, bark, stems, buds, seeds and fruit of
aromatic tropical plants.

Herbs and Spices:	Use in these foods:
Allspice	stews, soups, ground meats, barbecue sauce, tomatoes
Almond extract	fruits, puddings
Basil	beef, lamb, seafoods, soups, stews, stewed or fresh tomatoes
Bay leaves	meats, poultry, soups, stews, spaghetti dishes
Caraway seeds	meats, salads, breads, stews, asparagus, cabbage
Chives	salads, sauces, soups, stews, fish, meats, vegetables
Celery seed	meat loaf, cole slaw, soups
Cinnamon	fruits (especially apples), breads, pork, fish, squash, sweet potatoes
Chili powder	ground meats, casseroles, seafood, corn, French dressing

Herbs and Spices:	Use in these foods:
Cloves	fruits, roasted meats, baked fish, squash
Curry powder	lamb, chicken, fish, beef, vegetables
Dill weed	soups, salads, fish, meat, chicken, carrots, peas, zucchini
Garlic (not the salt)	casseroles, meats, salads, vegetables, tomato dishes
Ginger	chicken, oriental vegetables, fruits
Lemon or Lime juice	vegetables, meats, fish, seafoods, salads, fruit
Mace	hot breads, fruits salads, fish, veal
Marjoram	lamb, salmon, eggplant, green salads
Mint	fruit cups, veal, lamb, fish, sauces, green peas
Mustard (dry)	ground meats, fish, salads, sauces, beans
Nutmeg	cottage cheese, eggs, fruits, vegetables
Onion (not the salt)	meats, fish, vegetables, salads, tomatoes
Oregano	soups, stews, Italian casseroles, steaks, seafoods, tomatoes
Paprika	chicken, fish, meats, baked potatoes, cole slaw, wax beans
Pepper or Peppercorns	soups, stews, meats, chicken, vegetables, dressings
Peppermint extract	fruits, puddings
Pimento	salads, vegetable combinations, casseroles
Rosemary	meats, fish, poultry, dressings, potatoes, peas
Sage	poultry, meat, stuffings, rice, stews, green beans, tomatoes
Savory	scrambled eggs, soups, pork, ground meats, vegetables
Sherry (not cooking)	cream sherry: fruits dry sherry: soups, stews
Tarragon	soups, salads, meats, chicken, greens
Thyme	chicken, veal, pork, soups, salads, onions, tomatoes
Tumeric	meats, fish, sauces, rice

Note: Herb and Spice Guide courtesy of the Nutrition Section—Health Education Department, Park Nicollet Medical Foundation.

When experimenting with new flavorings, begin by using no more than one or two herbs or spices at a time. Start with small amounts: add ¼ teaspoon of dried herbs or 1 teaspoon of chopped fresh seasonings to soups and stews during the last hour of cooking. Adding them sooner will destroy the flavor. However, in cold dressings, dips, or marinades, add herbs and spices several hours before serving to "blend" the flavors.

As a general rule, use ¼ teaspoon of dried herbs for every four servings of food. You may want to try fresh herbs; some people find the flavor more lively than dried herbs. You can use fresh herbs even in recipes that call for dried herbs: substitute three to four times as much of the fresh herb as the dried herb. For example, if your recipe calls for 1 teaspoon of a dried herb, use 3 or 4 teaspoons of the fresh herb.

Salt substitutes

Salt substitutes taste like salt but contain little or no sodium. However, these products usually contain potassium chloride. The taste is bitter to some people, so try using a smaller amount than usual. Experiment with different brands to find what you like best.

Light salts are half sodium chloride and half potassium chloride.

People with kidney disease need to be careful about using products containing potassium chloride. If the kidneys aren't working well, potassium can build up in the bloodstream. Check with your doctor before using potassium chloride if you have kidney disease.

Even though salt substitutes may be fine to use, you probably will do better by cutting back on salt substitutes as well as salt. After a while, you'll probably find you don't miss the taste.

Modifying recipes

We often assume homemade items have much less sodium than commercial foods. That's usually true, but homemade items also can be loaded with sodium. For example:

1 cup homemade chow mein = 998 milligrams of sodium
1 cup commerical chow mein = 1380 milligrams of sodium

1 cup homemade beef stew = 730 mg. of sodium
1 cup canned beef stew = 989 mg. of sodium

You can modify homemade foods by omitting salt and salty ingredients, by substituting salt-free or reduced-sodium products and by adding herbs, spices, vinegars and other flavoring agents, as we said earlier. The chart on the next page will help you.

The first step in modifying a recipe is to identify the ingredients that contribute sodium. The second step is to decide how to eliminate the product or find a substitute. It's a good idea to check your supermarket or grocery store for reduced-sodium products. Manufacturers have begun making many items in low-sodium versions.

A Guide to Low Sodium Substitutes.

Common ingredient	Sodium in milligrams per serving	Possible substitute
Salt	1 tsp = 2300	See herb/spice guide or use salt substitute
Seasoned salt	1 tsp = 1610	See herb/spice guide or use commercial herb and spice blend
Garlic/onion salt	1 tsp = 1840	Garlic/onion powder Fresh garlic/onion
Canned vegetables	½ cup = 200-500	Fresh or frozen vegetables Canned salt-free vegetables
Canned soup	1 cup reconstituted = 966	Low-sodium or reduced sodium soup or home-made white sauce
Bouillon cubes	1 = 966	Low-sodium or reduced sodium bouillon
Cooking wine	¼ cup = 138	Drinking wine
Seasoned bread crumbs	1 cup = 2116	Unseasoned bread crumbs
Baking powder	1 tsp = 322	Potassium chloride baking powder (available through pharmacies)
Baking soda	1 tsp = 966	Potassium chloride baking soda
Soy sauce	1 tsp = 460	Low-sodium soy sauce
Processed cheese	1 oz = 405	See "milk" guide for lower sodium cheeses
Breakfast cereals	varies	Choose low-sodium cereals

To show you how simple modifying recipes can be, here's a recipe for spaghetti with meatballs modified to reduce the sodium content. The salt has been omitted, and sodium-free canned tomato products have been substituted. The spices are adequate for seasoning, so you don't need to add more. The sodium content of the original recipe was 932 milligrams per serving. The modified recipe has 133 milligrams. (Figures are for one serving or ⅛ of the recipe.)

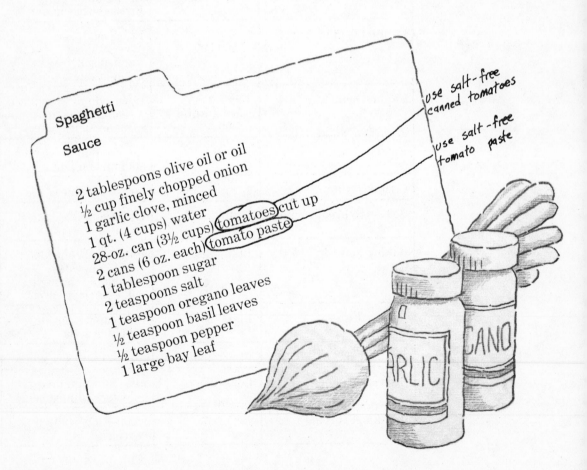

Spaghetti

Sauce

2 tablespoons olive oil or oil
½ cup finely chopped onion
1 garlic clove, minced
1 qt. (4 cups) water
28-oz. can (3½ cups) tomatoes cut up
2 cans (6 oz. each) tomato paste
1 tablespoon sugar
2 teaspoons salt
1 teaspoon oregano leaves
1 teaspoon basil leaves
½ teaspoon pepper
½ teaspoon pepper
1 large bay leaf

use salt-free canned tomatoes

use salt-free tomato paste

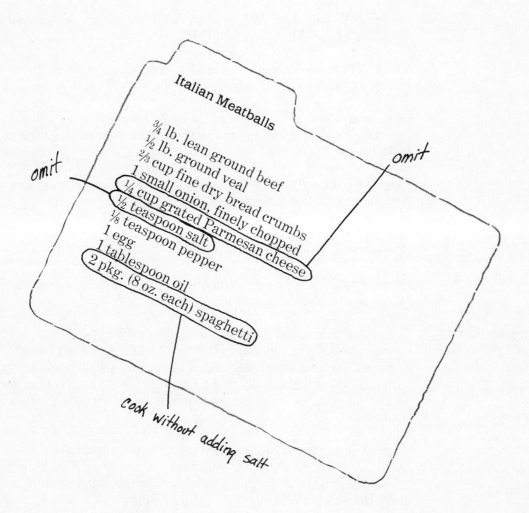

Italian Meatballs

¾ lb. lean ground beef
½ lb. ground veal
⅔ cup fine dry bread crumbs
1 small onion, finely chopped
¼ cup grated Parmesan cheese
½ teaspoon salt
⅛ teaspoon pepper
1 egg
1 tablespoon oil
2 pkg. (8 oz. each) spaghetti

omit

omit

Cook without adding salt

Cookbooks

With creative use of salt-free products, spices, and herbs, you can modify almost any recipe. Some trial and error will probably be necessary. To make the challenge easier, we've included a list of our favorite low-sodium cookbooks.

We think you'll enjoy many of these recipes.

Cooking Without Your Salt Shaker, American Heart Association, Northeast Ohio Affiliate, Inc., 1978.

Craig Clairborne's Gourmet Diet by Craig Clairborne with Pierre Franey. Ballentine Books, Inc. New York, 1981.

Deliciously Low, The Gourmet Guide to Low-Sodium, Low-Fat, Low-Cholesterol, Low-Sugar Cooking, New American Library, 1984.

Family Cookbook, Vol. II, American Diabetes Association and American Dietetic Association.

Low Salt Cooking, Better Homes and Gardens, Meredith Corporation, Des Moines, Iowa, 1983.

Pillsbury Kitchen's Family Cookbook, The Pillsbury Company, Minneapolis, Minnesota, 1979.

Low-sodium meal planning

Does all of this sound like too much work? We appreciate how overwhelming it might seem. But remember, you don't have to change all your eating habits right away. Start with a few easy adjustments and gradually add a few more. With a little practice, you'll find yourself choosing low-sodium foods without a second thought.

To show how easy it can be, here are two samples of a day's choices for three meals and two snacks. Compare the sodium levels and you'll see the difference! Notice the lower sodium menu doesn't include any out-of-the-ordinary foods. You're probably eating these foods now.

Compare these two menus:

	Milligrams of sodium		Milligrams of sodium
Breakfast		**Breakfast**	
¾ cup Rice Krispies	340	½ cup oatmeal	1
1 English muffin	365	2 slices toast	260
4 oz. tomato juice	335	4 oz. grapefruit juice	1
2 tsp. margarine	90	2 tsp. margarine	90
1 cup skim milk	125	1 cup skim milk	125
Coffee	2	Coffee	2
Total	1,257	Total	478
Snack		**Snack**	
Doughnut	140	Orange	1
Coffee	2		
Total	142	Total	1
Lunch		**Lunch**	
1 cup tomato soup	875	Salad with 1 Tbsp. Italian dressing	125
Sandwich:		Sandwich:	
2 slices of bread	260	2 slices of bread	260
1 oz. lunch meat	230	1 oz. turkey	30
1 oz. American cheese	405	Lettuce, tomato	10
1 Tbsp. mayonnaise	105	1 Tbsp. mayonnaise	105
½ dill pickle	715	Carrot sticks	25
⅛ apple pie	620	2 chocolate chip cookies	75
1 cup skim milk	125	1 cup skim milk	125
Total	3,335	Total	755
Dinner		**Dinner**	
3 oz. cured ham	675	3 oz. beef filet	60
½ cup au gratin potato	500	1 baked potato	5
½ cup fresh brocolli	10	½ cup fresh brocolli	10
1 refrigerator roll	335	1 roll	120
1 tsp. margarine	45	1 tsp. margarine	45
1/12 cake with icing	300	½ cup ice milk	53
Tea	15	Tea	15
Total	1,880	Total	308
Snack		**Snack**	
1 oz. chips	213	3 cups popcorn, unsalted	2
12 oz. regular pop	50	12 oz. diet pop	75
Total	264	Total	77
Day's total	6,877	Day's total	1,619

Want to try your own menu? Here's a guide to help you. You might want to record a menu based on your present eating habits and another using the low-sodium options. (Feel free to photo copy these pages to use in the future.)

SAMPLE MENU	Milligrams of Sodium
BREAKFAST	
_____	_____
_____	_____
_____	_____
_____	_____
_____	
MORNING SNACK	
_____	_____
_____	_____
_____	
LUNCH	
_____	_____
_____	_____
_____	_____
_____	
AFTERNOON SNACK	
_____	_____
_____	_____
DINNER	
_____	_____
_____	_____
_____	_____
_____	
BEDTIME SNACK	
_____	_____
_____	_____
_____	_____
TOTAL	_____

*You're on
Your Way*

We hope we've answered some of your questions about hypertension. More importantly, we hope we've given you some practical tips and guidelines for lowering the amount of sodium you eat.

Remember, you can adjust slowly. You don't have to change your eating habits overnight. Each small step will help.

We hope you'll soon discover a whole new world of tastes and seasonings as you say "Pass the Pepper Please!"

References

The American Diabetes Association and American Dietetic Association. A Nutrition Guide for Professionals: The Application of Exchange Lists for Meal Planning. Alexandria, Virginia: The American Diabetes Association, 1988.

Franz, Marion J., M.S., R.D. Fast Food Facts. Minneapolis, Minnesota: Diabetes Center, Inc., 1984, revised 1985, 1987.

Composition of Foods. Washington, D.C.: USDA, Agriculture Handbook No. 8-9, 1980.

Manual of Clinical Nutrition. Minneapolis, Minnesota: Twin Cities District Dietetic Association, 1988.

Monk, Arlene, R.D. and Marion J. Franz, M.S., R.D. Convenience Food Facts. Minneapolis, Minnesota: Diabetes Center, Inc., 1984, revised 1985, 1987.

Pillsbury Kitchen's Family Cookbook. Minneapolis, Minnesota: The Pillsbury Company, 1979.

The Sodium Content of Your Food. USDA, Home and Garden Bulletin No. 233, 1983.

Appendix

What are the Exchange Lists?

The sodium content lists in this book are organized into exchange lists based on the *Exchange Lists for Meal Planning*, a widely used guide to meal planning for people with diabetes or anyone interested in a healthful eating plan. Exchange lists help people eat a nutritionally balanced diet and include a wide variety of foods without having to count calories.

There are six exchange lists:

1. starch/bread
2. meat
3. vegetable
4. fruit
5. milk
6. fat

Exchange lists contain measured portions, or servings, of food which may be substituted, traded, or exchanged for other food items within the same list. All of the foods on each list have similar amounts of carbohydrate, protein, fat, and calories. Specific serving sizes are listed for each food, and substitutes must be made in the amount specified.

People with diabetes use a meal plan to outline the number of exchanges from each food list to eat at meals and snacks. People with hypertension may use a meal plan to help them lose weight and to reduce sodium intake, which are both important steps in controlling high blood pressure. A meal plan is individualized according to each person's lifestyle, age, weight, sex, activity level, and what kinds of medications they may be taking. Everyone can use a meal plan to help ensure a balanced diet and maintain a consistent calorie intake each day.

To obtain an individualized meal plan using exchanges, contact a Registered Dietitian (R.D.) in your area. An R.D. can assess your current eating habits, recommend changes to help you achieve your nutritional goals, and determine an appropriate calorie level for you.

For more information on the Exchange Lists, write to the American Dietetic Association, 208 South La Salle Street, Suite 1100, Chicago, Illinois 60604 or to the American Diabetes Association, Diabetes Information Service Center, 1660 Duke Street, Alexandria, Virginia 22314.